Meandering Pub V

Chapters

(1)   Denbury   4.5 miles   The Union Inn

(2)   Christow   3.5 miles Artichoke Inn

(3)   Ilsington   4.5 miles   Carpenters Arms

(4)   Luton   5 miles   The Elizabethan

(5)   Combeinteignhead 4 miles   Church House Inn

(6)   Hennock 4.5 miles   Palk Arms

(7)   Chudleigh 3.5 to 6 miles   Bishop Lacey

(8)   Churston Ferrers   3 miles   Churston Court Hotel

(9)   Doddiscombsleigh   4 miles Nobody Inn

(10)   North Bovey   3 miles Ring of Bells

DISCLAIMER

The contents of the book are correct at time of publication. However we cannot be held responsible for any errors or omissions or changes in details or for any consequences of any reliance on the information provided. We have tried to be accurate in the book, but things can change and would be grateful if readers advise us of any inaccuracies they may encounter.

We have taken every care to ensure the walks are safe and achievable by walkers with a reasonable level of fitness. But with outdoor activities there is always a degree of risk involved and the publisher accepts no responsibility for any injury caused to readers while following these walks.

SAFETY FIRST

All the walks have been covered to ensure minimum risk to walkers that follow the routes.

Always be particularly careful if crossing main roads, but remember traffic can also be dangerous even on minor country lanes.

If in the country and around farms be careful of farm machinery and livestock (take care to put dog on lead) and observe the **Country Code**.

Also ensure you wear suitable clothing and footwear, I would advise wearing walking boots which protect from wet feet and add extra ankle support over uneven terrain.

There are a few rules that should be observed if walking alone advise somebody were you are walking and approximate time you will return. Allow plenty of time for the walk especially if it is further and or more difficult than you have walked before. Whatever the distance make sure you have enough daylight hours to complete the walk safely. When walking along a country road always walk on the right to face oncoming traffic, the only exception is on a blind bend were you cross to the left to have a clear view and can be seen from both directions.

If bad weather should come in making visibility difficult, do not panic just try to remember any features along route and get out the map to pinpoint the area but be sure before you move off, that you are moving in the right direction.

Unfortunately accidents can still happen even on the easiest of walks, if this is the case make sure the person in trouble is safe before seeking help. If carrying a mobile phone dial 999 or 112 European Union emergency number will connect you to any network to get you help.

Unmapped walks we recommend that you take the relevant Ordnance Survey map and compass with you, even if you have a Smartphone, digi-walker or G.P.S all of which can fail on route.

Introduction

This book contains 10 circular walks that offer great countryside, quiet country lanes, green lanes and open fields. Some of the walks are in Doddiscombsleigh, Christow, North Bovey, Churston Ferrers and Luton which can be walked through all the seasons in the year, but there can be some muddy sections so on all walks wear the correct footwear like walking boots to keep your feet dry and give support to ankles. The Inn's selected are some of the finest in Devon both for the food and there real ale. The walks are between 3 and 5 miles and if you want to check out the extra photos on U Tube showing the countryside then select Meandering Pub Walks in Devon.

A lot of the Inns are tucked away in the country nestling under hills and surrounded by green valleys to help find them if you have a Sat Nav I have added the post code which will make it easier for location. Please do not park in the pub car parks without the permission of the Landlord.

In most of these pubs well behaved dogs are welcome which like for me is very important to keep our four legged friends happy with a drink and maybe a snack after a long walk.

Good luck to all you walkers and families with the dogs, the Devon country side is beautiful but please remember let us all keep it that way so take rubbish home and do not leave bottles or plastic containers, remember keep it for the younger families for the next century it is really worth the time just to clear up.

Please if you do have dogs then follow the country code in spring and summer for the safety of you the dog and the farm animals. Keep all those gates shut and stay on the footpaths

Because these walks are in most cases way out in the country then the car is the only form of transport. I hope you enjoy the walking experience and keep a look out for the unexpected like Alpaca in the Devon Countryside what a beautiful and curious animal they are and so friendly.

Check out the other eBooks/paperback in the Meandering Walking Series;
Meandering in Mid Devon
Meandering in South Devon
Meandering on Rivers and Canals in Devon
Look out for the next eBook/paperback later in 2014 or early 2015
Meandering Tea Room Walks in Devon.

Happy Walking

Meandering Pub Walks in Devon

Chapter 1   Denbury   Union Inn

Park & Start Grid ref;   SX 823686   Post Code; TQ12 6DQ

Distance: 4.5 miles

Level;   Easy

Time: 1 hour 30 minutes

Terrain: Mostly country lanes and green lanes with the path through the centre of the Old Iron Age Fort high above Denbury.

Maps.   O.S Explorer 114 Torquay and Dawlish

Refreshments: Union Inn

Amber in the Iron Age Hill Fort above Denbury.

Union Inn Denbury

The Pub

The Union Inn is a traditional 14th century Inn which overlooks the village green. The interior is a brown and cream décor with glorious roaring log fires. The bar is very relaxing with its comfy leather sofas and you can also enjoy the light bites. In the restaurant which changes its menu on a regular basis depending on the seasons. This can be fish, game, meat and vegetarian dishes which are all obtained locally.

Check the web; www.theunioninndenbury.co.uk for events and offers.

Opening times

12 pm – 3 pm and 6 pm – 11 pm Monday to Thursday.

All day Friday to Sunday

Food served Daily 12.00 – 2.30 pm and 6.30 to 9.30 pm.

Access to start

Leave Newton Abbot on the Totnes road A381, then at roundabout at Ogwell take second exit on to Ogwell Road, from here follow signpost into Denbury.

The Walk

(1)

The walk starts from the green outside the Union Inn, take the lane to the right of the pub as you look from the front and continue along lane for about half mile to Wrenwell Cross. At the crossroad follow lane to the right in the direction of Woodland taking time to look at the views out over the surrounding countryside. Then at the next crossroads turn right which is signposted to Denbury and follow the lane taking in the great views out to Haytor, you then start to go through a series of bends, then as you are just coming out the last bend there is a large gate set back off the road in the hedge on the right, this is just before a lane on left down to Norden Farm.

(2)

Do not go as far as the lane but go through gate on right and start to climb 15 metres up the field to a stile tucked back in the right hand corner. Go over stile into the woods and follow path up hill to reach a sign that indicates the entrance to the Old Iron Age Hill Fort, continue along the pathway through some of the 9 acres of wood to the gate at the end. Go through gate and follow the track all the way downhill to the bottom to reach a country lane. Turn right on lane and follow the lane straight through part of the village ignoring all road junctions along the way to reach the centre of the village at the crossroads. Turn right at this point and follow lane back to the Green in front of the Union Inn.

Overlooking Denbury just below Iron Age Hill Fort.

Chapter 2   Christow   Artichoke Inn

Park & Start Grid ref; SX 837850   Post Code; EX6 7NF

Distance: 3.5 miles

Level;   Moderate

Time: 1 hour 45 minutes

Terrain: The walk is mostly country lanes which makes it suitable for an all season walk but at the start of the walk there is a very steep uphill climb for almost a mile.

Maps.   O.S Explorer 110 Torquay and Dawlish

Refreshments: Artichoke Inn

Wood that backs onto Canonteign House and Country Park.

Artichoke Inn   Christow

The Pub

The Artichoke Inn is a magnificent 12th century Inn with a delightful thatched roof and mis-shaped walls which goes back to when the Crusaders would have visited. This is in the centre of Christow in the beautiful Teign Valley on the very edge of Dartmoor. The interior is the image of a great olde world charm very fitting for a 12th century Inn, with log fire and dark wooden sitting.

The menu is varied and extensive so check the web for the full range.
www.theartichokeinn.co.uk

Opening times

Open 6 days a week closed on Mondays
Tuesday – Saturday 12.00 – 2.30 pm   5.30 – 11 pm
Sunday open 12.00 – 10.30 pm.

Access to start

Take the Exeter to Plymouth A38 and exit at slip road to Chudleigh turn right of slip road then second right onto B3193 follow road up the Teign Valley to signpost marked Christow.

The Walk

(1)

The walk starts in the car park off Village Road near the Community Centre. Exit car park and turn left following Village Road uphill heading into the centre of Christow. After passing the church and after about another half mile you will reach the Artichoke Inn on the left just before a road junction. Keep over to the right ignoring lane off to the left staying on Village Road around bend, then after about 250 metres the road splits and starts to rise with Wet Lane straight ahead. At this point take the road junction off to the left marked Dry Lane staying on this lane for nearly 2 miles rising up hill all the time to the very top. At the top go past Heckland Farm on right and then through several bends on lane (at this point there is a public footpath straight through field which cuts the corner off lane but this can be very muddy). If you continue on lane you go past a no through road off to the right this leads up through woods down to Kennick Reservoir at **SX 817847** but to continue walk just stay on lane and follow to end to a road junction.

(2)

Turn left at junction and follow lane all the way downhill just ignore all other road junctions off to the left midway down the hill and continue on down to the bottom to reach a road junction signposted Chudleigh and Ashton. Turn left at junction and follow the lane along to Combe Cross keeping over to the left, you then start to rise up the hill then after about half mile you will reach the Christow sign on left next to Bennah Hill junction. Ignore the junction and just carry straight on to reach a fork junction in road. Keep over to the right down past a house on junction the fork with its entrance in Church Lane. Follow Church Lane to the end and at the junction turn right which brings you back onto Village Road walk past the church and return to the car park.

Chapter 3   Ilsington   Carpenters Arms

Park & Start Grid ref;   SX 785760   Post Code;   TQ13 9RG

Distance: 5 miles

Level;   Moderate

Time: 2 hours

Terrain: This walk takes you through the woods and along green lanes through the quiet country lanes and up over a very large hill.

Maps.   O.S Explorer 110 Torquay and Dawlish

Refreshments: Carpenters Arms.

A quiet babbling brook along a tranquil walk.

Carpenters Arms

The Pub

The Carpenters Arms is tucked away behind the church in the centre of Ilsington village within the Dartmoor National Park. It is a very quiet location were children and families are welcome along with well-behaved dogs. The interior is well set out and finished with a lot of charm. There is also a small beer garden out the front of the Inn. The Carpenters Arms is thought to have been a farmhouse which then became a public house in about 1816. The food is good and again very varied check the website www.thecarpentersarms.co.uk

Opening times
Monday to Thursday 12pm – 3 pm / 6pm – 11 pm
Friday 12 pm -3 pm / 6 pm – 12 am
Saturday 12 pm – 12 am   Sunday 10 pm
Food served Daily 12 pm – 2 pm / 6pm – 9 pm (Sunday 8 pm).

Access to start
Leave A38 Exeter to Plymouth road off slipway to Bovey Tracey at Drumbridges roundabout take the third exit then follow sign to Liverton at next junction go onto the Old Liverton Road and follow straight through to Ilsington then at church go left onto Old Town Hill.

The Walk

(1)

Try and park near the Carpenters Arms on the lane and then walk down Old Town Hill, go past Town Meadow on your right and the little community shop, then just at the brow of the hill on the edge of the woods turn left into woods. Stay on path in woods and follow straight downhill ignoring all other paths, go to the bottom and exit onto lane. Cross lane with care and go straight up lane directly opposite and follow up hill to reach Woodhouse Cross at top of hill. Once at the crossroads turn right down Tipleyhill Lane a green lane and continue for over a mile to the end ignoring any turns along the way. At the end turn right onto the road on the outskirts of Liverton, then after a few metres at road junction turn right again onto the main road out of Liverton on to Ilsington. Take care on this section traffic at times can be busy, but continue to follow the road past the Old Mill on right, then at this point you can extend the walk by going left and follow the track opposite the mill on through Rora Wood and then on through East Lounston.

(2)

If you choose to stay on the lane then continue on for a few metres to reach a lane that goes off to left at Willis Cross which is mark Lounston. This goes through Lower Lounston passing the nature reserve on the left along the way, just continue along the lane ignoring all turnings to finally reach Five Cross Roads. Turn right at this point and walk up hill for nearly a mile to reach Swinepark Cross, turn right down narrow lane and follow for about another mile past house on right marked Wottonbury staying on lane for about 1 mile back into Ilsington at junction turn right which leads back to the Carpenters Arms.

Chapter 4   **Luton**   **Elizabethan Inn**

Park & Start Grid ref;   SX 902769   **Post Code; TQ13 0BL**

Distance: 5 miles

Level;   Easy

Time: 1 hour 45 minutes

Terrain: There are a couple of steep climbs along the way with country lanes narrow tracks and green lanes.

Maps.   O.S Explorer 110 Torquay and Dawlish

Refreshments: Elizabethan Inn

The small brook as it runs down through the meadows in the valley.

Elizabethan Inn

The Pub

The Elizabethan Inn is in the heart of a quaint little hamlet set underneath Haldon Hill. The food and ale were highly noted by the Good Food Guide. Many of the dishes are traditional classics but adding an extra touch of class to excite the palate. There are both a set menu and a la carte which changes on a regular basis. The original Inn dates back to the 16th century and the interior is well balanced between contemporary and traditional features. There is also original beams which blends with the classic wood burning stove. The Elizabethan Inn was original called The Albert but in about 1952 the name of the then Heavitree House was changed. The new owners wrote to our present Queen Elizabeth II after her coronation to get permission to rename it the Elizabethan.

Opening times

Pub and Restaurant
Monday to Friday 12 pm – 3 pm / 6 pm – 11 pm
Saturday and Sunday 12 pm – 11 pm.

Access to start
Turn off the A380 Exeter to Torquay road at Wapperwell Dip go down slip road and turn right go under Ideford Arch turn left at road junction and follow road then through Ideford on into Luton.

The Walk

(1)

The walk starts at lane near to the Elizabethan Inn car park. Exit car park onto Fore Street and follow lane all the way through the little hamlet of Luton up the hill past the farm and buildings on both sides of the road. At the top of the hill there is a sharp left hand bend, go around bend ignoring road junction on right. After 25 metres the main lane continues around to the right at Luton Cross but you walk straight ahead down a lane past the riding stables on the right. Follow lane to the bottom of the dip to a road junction the main lane swings off to the left but you turn right on the lane signposted Kingsteignton. Once on lane it starts to rise and at the first bend there is a narrow track off to the left, ignore track but just a few metres on there is a wider track on right. Turn right and follow green lane to the end. At the end you reach a junction with Town Farm Lane and a barn conversion on left go straight across lane onto another green lane which is Hamblecombe Lane.

(2)

Follow Hamblecombe Lane for about 1 mile up hill to the end, then exit briefly onto Orchard Lane, keep right to reach the main lane through to Ideford. At this point you can shorten walk by just following lane back through Ideford on to Luton. To continue the main walk cross Ideford Lane onto a small track called Haldon Lane and continue as it rises steeply in places to the end. Turn right onto Bowden Lane and follow back downhill into the centre of Ideford past the church on the right on down to the road junction. Turn left at junction and carry on through Ideford back up to Luton Cross then retrace your steps back into Luton to the Elizabethan Inn.

Chapter 5   Combeinteignhead   Wild Goose Inn

Park & Start Grid ref;   SX 899716   Post Code; TQ12 4RA

Distance: 4 miles

Level;   Moderate

Time: 2 hours

Terrain: This is a walk of country lanes and green lanes with great 360 degree views once at the top of the hill. There are a couple of steep climbs.

Maps.   O.S Explorer 110 Torquay and Dawlish

Refreshments: Wild Goose Inn

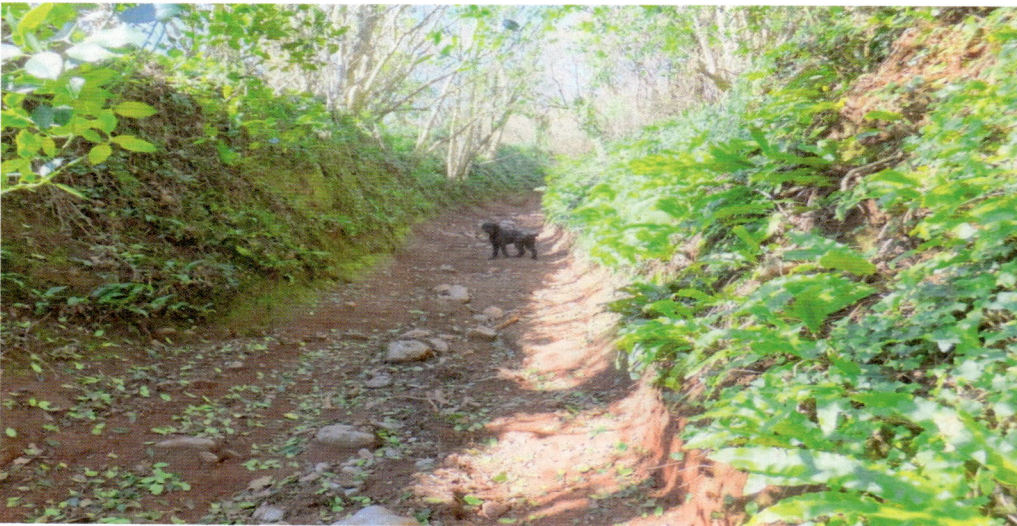

Amber on the green lane out of Middle Rocombe.

Wild Goose Inn

The Pub

The Wild Goose Inn is a family owned pub which is situated in the valley running down to the River Teign. The Wild Goose Inn became a public house in 1840 which was then then called the Country House Inn, it was renamed in the 1960's when a local farmers geese would attack customers on arriving and leaving the premises. The interior is charming which fits in with its period, and there is also a walled garden at back which is sunny and in a nice sheltered position. The Wild Goose Inn was awarded Runner-Up in the 2012 South Devon Pub of the Year. The food is very good with a good variation and all produce source locally. Check website www.thewildgooseinn.co.uk

Opening times

Monday to Saturday 11 am – 3 pm / 5.30 pm – 11 pm
(Midnight Friday and Saturday) Sunday 12 pm – 3 pm / 7 pm – 11 pm.

Access to start

At Penn Inn roundabout on the A380 Exeter to Torquay turn left at the traffic lights onto Shaldon Road go straight up over Cross Hill and follow road right on into Combeinteignhead.

The Walk

(1)

The walk starts at the car park as you enter Combeinteignhead from Newton Abbot on the Shaldon Road. Exit car park turning left and follow Shaldon Road around to road junction. Turn right at junction leaving the Shaldon Road walk up past the Wild Goose Inn on right in village and follow lane out into the countryside then after about a mile you reach a sign welcome to Stokeinteignhead. With the road junction just before sign turn right this is marked Rocombe, then continue to follow lane for almost a mile to enter Middle Rocombe, just as you enter hamlet there is Middle Rocombe Farm on left and directly opposite is a green lane on right signposted Coffinswell/ Kingskerswell. Follow the green lane as it climbs very steeply to the very top of hill to reach a lane.

(2)

Turn right onto lane and follow around down past Mount Olive on the right, be sure to soak up the views from up on top the hill before reaching a house set back from the lane on the right with a large tree on a green outside the entrance to the house. Then off to the right hidden behind the tree is a green lane which twist and turns down the hill with views out over the Teign Estuary to finally after about a mile reach the Shaldon Road in Combeinteignhead. Turn left at road to return to the car park or right if you are in need of refreshments at the Wild Goose Inn.

Park & Start Grid ref;   SX 833808   Post Code; TQ13 9QB

Distance: 4.5 miles

Level;   Moderate

Time: 2 hours

Terrain: Country lanes but some very steep climbs, also along green lanes and maybe slight detour to view reservoirs up on top hill.

Maps.   O.S Explorer 110 Torquay and Dawlish

Refreshments: Palk Arms

Great view down over the wooded valley leading back to Hennock.

Palk Arms

The Pub

The Palk Arms is a 16th century Free House pub, this sits high above the Teign Valley overlooking a patchwork quilt of green fields and rolling hills. The pub is situated on land once owned by the wealthy Palk family and possibly sited on what was, a very long time ago the village green. The layout of the pub as changed many times over the years but when you once walked in the entrance the bar and drinking areas were on the left, and the large fireplace on the right in the owner's front room. It goes without saying that a place this old also as its share of ghosts. The menu is very varied and caters for all. To be sure check the website www.thepalkarms.co.uk

Opening times
Monday closed all day
Tuesday to Thursday 6 pm -11 pm   Friday 5 pm – 11 pm
Saturday 12 pm – 11 pm.

Access to start

Leave A38 Exeter to Plymouth road at Chudleigh slip road and follow road through into Chudleigh Knighton exit onto Bovey Tracey road then once out of Chudleigh Knighton follow sign for Hennock.

The Walk

(1)

The walk starts off in Hennock where ever you can park near to the Palk Arms. Then from the Palk Arms take Bell Lane opposite pub and start to walk up hill past the old church on the right and continue on lane for a mile to a road junction off to left. Turn left and follow Bowden Lane to the end to a road junction, turn right and follow up hill for half mile to another road junction and turn left.

(2)

Continue on lane for just under a mile to reach Pool Mill Cross, if you follow main lane around to the left this takes you to the reservoirs but we go slightly to the right and straight ahead down no through lane next to the Water Board buildings on right. Follow lane downhill and past the old reservoir pumping house and the water overflow area to the end of the lane, then keep over to the left and go up a track with a slight slope to start levelling out further up the track (this section can be muddy) but follow to the end to join a lane.

(3)

Before turning right on main lane look back over Tottiford Reservoir, continue to walk down Beadon Lane for about 1.5 miles down through the beautiful wooded valley with the water running through the centre of the low laying area. But then it is a climb up and up to finally reach Cherrycombe Cross. Once at the cross turn left and head back down the hill finally arriving back at the Palk Arms.

Chapter 7   **Chudleigh**   **Bishop Lacey**

Park & Start Grid ref;   **SX 867795**   **Post Code; TQ13 0HY**

Distance: **3.5 miles**

Level; Easy

Time: **1 hour 30 minutes**

Terrain: **There is one steep climb and through green lanes and country lanes also the crossing of open fields with views over Chudleigh Rocks.**

Maps.   **O.S Explorer 110 Torquay and Dawlish**

Refreshments: **Bishop Lacey.**

The stream to the front of Lowell House.

Bishop Lacey

The Pub

The Bishop Lacey is partly 14th century low beam church house. The interior is of dark decoration with log fire, two bars and a dining room. There is good homemade food with nice staff and character locals. The original name of the pub was the Plymouth Inn which was changed in 1961. The Bishop Lacey comes from Edmund Lacey who was the Bishop of Exeter from 1420 to 1455, it is reputed that he was responsible for bringing fresh water supply to the town.

Opening times

Monday to Thursday   12 pm – 12 am
Friday and Saturday   12 pm – 1 am
Food served 12 pm – 2.30 pm / 6 pm – 9 pm
All day Sunday.

Access to start

Leave A38 Exeter to Plymouth road off slip road into Chudleigh, proceed through town were Bishop Lacey is on main road opposite the church.

The Walk

(1)

The walk starts in the car park in the centre of Chudleigh, exit car park and turn right onto Market Way walk to the road junction and turn right onto Old Exeter Street then after only a few metres turn left just before the War Memorial. Then cross the main road New Exeter Street into Clifford Street directly opposite and walk down lane past the Ship Inn. Stay on Clifford Street all the way to the bottom at the crossroads. Go straight ahead at crossroads still on Clifford Street over bridge and continue on up lane as it rises past the cemetery on the left just before a sharp left hand bend there is a driveway on right and next to it is a narrow path, take the path up a steep hill through the wooded area to the end to reach a lane at the top of the hill.

(2)

Turn right on lane and follow for about 1.5 miles with some spectacular views out over towards Haytor and on the left there is a brief glimpse of were Dykes Fort was many years ago. Continue on lane to the first junction off to the right, turn down right and follow lane downhill then were the lane veers around to the left go straight on down a green lane with Chudleigh Rocks ahead follow lane down to a large gate. Go through gate continue to follow track down to the left past Lowell House then over the bridge across the stream to a small gate off to the left. Again go through gate and follow path up through slightly over grown area to exit gate into field, then follow well defined path up to the left corner of field to exit via a kissing gate.

(3)

Once through gate you are on the main road, so cross carefully on to pavement on opposite side and follow up Station Road past the Old Police Station onto the Parade stay on the left and follow the road for half mile to Bishop Lacey on left and just past the pub and before the pedestrian crossing there is a small alley way off to the left that leads back into the car park.

Chapter 8   Churston Ferrers   Churston Court Inn

Park & Start Grid ref;   SX 904563   Post Code; TQ5 0JE

Distance: 3 miles

Level;   Easy

Time: 1 hour 30 minutes

Terrain: This is country lanes, South West Coast Path and down green lanes and through woods. There is also crossing stony coves and some open fields.

Maps.   O.S Explorer OL20 South Devon

Refreshments: Churston Court Inn

Churston Cove along the South West Coast Path.

Churston Court Inn

The Pub

The Churston Court Inn dates back to the 12th century as a grade I listed Manor House which is packed with history and original features. It goes without saying that a place this old also as its ghost, the most common being a monk that walks through walls? It has also been the place were some famous people have stayed like Sir Humphrey Gilbert and is half-brother Sir Walter Raleigh, and also Dame Agatha Christie wrote one of her books about Poirot during her stay. The food menu is very good from set menu to A la carte and the place is packed with atmosphere and character. Check website www.churstoncourtinn.co.uk

Opening times

Monday through to Sunday 10.00 am – Midnight.

Access to start
Follow A380 ring road towards Brixham turn right at Dartmouth Road, arriving at Galmpton continue on towards Brixham past Churston Farm Shop and Cayman Golf Club. Then take next left signposted to Churston Ferrers.

The Walk

(1)

The walk starts at or near the Churston Court Inn follow Church Lane around past the church following the lane around the next bend and up a slight slope, at top of slope the road swings off to the left but you go straight ahead on past Links Close and around to the right. Straight ahead is a sign that is marked Elberry Cove pointing down a narrow pathway, follow down to the left. Stay on path as you go right through the centre of the golf course, then when you drop down a slope take the path to the right through a wooded section and with a house on your left follow Elberry Lane to the end. At the end junction you can turn left for a detour into Broadsands, but for us we turn right and follow the South West Coast Path on into Elberry Cove with its little stone bathers changing room on left from way back.

(2)

Once having crossed the cove go up the steps on the opposite side and start to climb up the hill, at the junction about midway up follow the path to the left and continue to climb the hill to the top. Stay on the South West Coast Path on through to Churston Cove go down the steps then cross the cove and up the steps on the far side stay on the South West Coast Path up hill to the top. At the top there is a signpost marked Brixham or Churston Ferrers. We turn right and follow the track through the woods this then leads out into a open field, but stay on the track through a large gateway at the end of the field onto a enclosed track.

(3)

Follow the track for half mile to the end (part of this section maybe muddy). Once at the end crossover the step over stile out on to a lane, turn right and after just a few metres turn right at the road junction to see the Churston Court Inn straight in front of you.

Chapter 9   Doddiscombsleigh   Nobody Inn

Park & Start Grid ref;   SX 855866   Post Code; EX6 7PS

Distance: 4 miles

Level;   Easy

Time: 2 hours

Terrain: This is a walk for all seasons along country lanes, there is a very steep climb up towards Haldon Belvedere which is about a mile to the top.

Maps.   O.S Explorer 110 Torquay and Dawlish

Refreshments: Nobody Inn

Lawrence Tower or Haldon Belvedere.

Nobody Inn Doddiscombsleigh

The Pub

The Nobody Inn is set in Doddiscombsleigh between Haldon Hill and the Teign Valley. The 17th century Inn is just full of atmosphere and unspoilt charm through the years. It as low ceilings, blackened beams, inglenook fireplace and antique furniture. The menu is varied and exciting and there are over 250 wines and 240 whiskies mainly malt and ever increasing at cask strength. The earliest records of the area was before Domesday which named a Saxon as being landowner of Doddiscombsleigh. The Nobody Inn did not become an Inn until 1838, but however from the early 1600's it was virtually the village unofficial Church House. Check website www.nobodyinn.co.uk

Opening times

Bar Monday to Saturday 11 am – 11 pm Sunday 12 pm – 10.30 pm
Bar Meals Monday to Thursday 12 pm – 2 pm and 6.30 – 9 pm
Friday and Saturday 12 pm – 2 pm and 6.30 pm – 9.30 pm
Sunday 12 pm – 3 pm and 7 pm – 9 pm
Restaurant Tuesday to Saturday evening inclusive.

Access to start
Leave A38 at top of Haldon Hill before horse race course go under bridge and follow lane past Haldon Belvedere take second lane off to left and follow into

Doddiscombsleigh.

The Walk

(1)

The walk starts near the Nobody Inn in the centre of Doddiscombsleigh. Take the lane back in the direction of Exeter go past the bus shelter then on past the church on your right and ignore the road junction off to the left. The lane then reaches a sharp right hand bend with a farm entrance straight ahead go past the entrance on around onto Tick Lane. Stay on lane for about a mile rising up the whole time to finally reach a road junction, turn left at the junction and then continue to climb up hill again. Take time to look at the views on the way up and look out for Alpacas in the field near the top. Continue to climb hill to the top to reach a forked junction just below Lawrence Tower (Haldon Belvedere).

(2)

Go left at the road junction and follow the road across the top of the ridge with magnificent views out over to the left down the valley back towards Doddiscombsleigh. Then at the first road junction on the left, turn down and follow lane past Willhayes Farm on the left and then after about another half mile you will reach Willhayes Cross. Turn left at the cross with the signpost marked Doddiscombsleigh and head off down Willhayes Hill, follow for nearly a mile to reach road junctions and bridleway follow the lane as it sweeps around to the left marked to Doddiscombsleigh then follow all the way to the end to a road junction.

(3)

Turn right at the road junction and follow lane back to the Nobody Inn for a well-deserved rest and good refreshments.

Chapter 10   North Bovey   Ring of Bells

Park & Start Grid ref;   SX 740839   **Post Code; TQ13 8RB**

Distance: 3 miles

Level; Easy

Time: 1 hour 30 minutes

Terrain: The walk is a mix of country lanes, green lanes and a track through Bovey Castle golf course.

Maps.   O.S Explorer OL28 Dartmoor

Refreshments: Ring of Bells

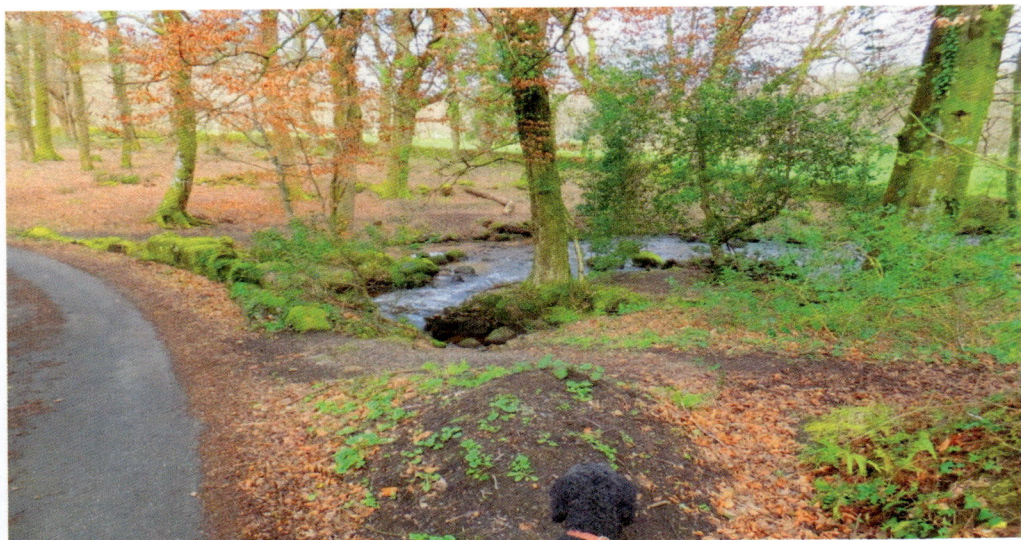

River Bovey.

Ring of Bells   North Bovey

The Pub

The Ring of Bells is a magnificent thatched Dartmoor Inn with many period features which include a 15th century arched door frame, low ceilings and beams and there is a grandfather clock built into the wall. Its rooms are heated by open fires and in the evenings candle light is added to give it that warm welcome atmosphere. The original building was built back in the 13th century to house the stonemasons who built the local church. The food is very good and the menu are varied to please all taste. Check website www.theringofbells.co.uk

Opening times

Open all year round
10 am – 11 pm Serve coffee at 10 am
Food is served
Lunch 12 pm – 2.30 pm
Evening 6 pm – 9 pm

Access to start
Take M5 or A38 and drive to Moretonhampstead, then from centre of town follow sign to North Bovey.

The Walk

(1)

The walk starts from the green next to the Ring of Bells, then walk down lane in the direction of the church and at road junction turn left. Then after just a few metres take the narrow path off to the right marked to Blackaller and follow all the way to the end. On exit from path turn left and follow lane over the bridge across the River Bovey. Then just stay on lane up the hill for about half mile the road then veers around to the left at this point take the lane off to the right and look out over the gate to get your first glimpse of Bovey Castle a very magnificent hotel. Stay on this lane for about a mile going down through a beautiful wooded area over a bridge crossing the River Bovey again with Bovey Castle golf course on the right.

(2)

Once over the bridge look out for a large gate set in the wall which leads into the golf course this is marked with a sign to North Bovey. Go through gate and follow track (please be sure to stay on track and look out for flying golf balls). Follow the track keeping left at junction at top of hill to go past the Manor Court on the left, with the entrance up in the distance take the lane in that direction but after just a few metres take the marked footpath to the right across the fairway to exit gate on to a lane. Turn right on lane and follow down a slope past the main entrance to Bovey Castle stay on lane up the hill to reach a road junction after nearly a mile.

(3)

Turn right at junction and follow lane ignoring all other junctions just keep straight on to reach the North Bovey sign then drop down the hill and were the road forks keep over to the left (depending on where you parked) and retrace your steps back to the car and refreshments in the Ring of Bells.

9282454R00021

Printed in Great Britain
by Amazon.co.uk, Ltd.,
Marston Gate.